Fundamentals of Faith

Bob Jones

BOB JONES UNIVERSITY PRESS, INC.
Greenville, South Carolina 29614

Fundamentals of Faith
Seventh Printing
ISBN 0-89084-140-3

TABLE OF CONTENTS

INTRODUCTION

At every week-day chapel and at every Sunday morning service, the students and faculty of Bob Jones University recite the "Bob Jones University Creed"—a formulated statement which embodies the fundamental doctrines of the Christian faith and which is a part of the second paragraph of the University Charter. The University would not retain in its employ any person who could not subscribe to the spirit and words of this statement.

Because of its doctrinal importance and its value in setting forth the scriptural position of this Christian University, we decided to put into print a series of chapel messages which explain our Creed in simple language. We want our friends away from the University as well as our faculty and students to know the implications in every phrase.

This Creed sets forth the great fundamentals of the faith held by all Bible believers. Godly Christians may differ on what the Scripture teaches about some things and may not agree on the interpretation of certain doctrines; but upon the great fundamental truths set forth in the "Bob Jones University Creed," they are in complete agreement. These are the essential doctrines, the foundation of Christian faith.

EXCERPT FROM THE BOB JONES UNIVERSITY CHARTER

The general nature and object of the corporation shall be to conduct an institution of learning for the general education of youth in the essentials of culture and in the arts and sciences, giving special emphasis to the Christian religion and the ethics revealed in the Holy Scriptures; combating all atheistic, agnostic, pagan, and so-called scientific adulterations of the gospel; unqualifiedly affirming and teaching:

The inspiration of the Bible, both the Old and the New Testaments; the creation of man by the direct act of God; the incarnation and virgin birth of our Lord and Saviour, Jesus Christ; His identification as the Son of God; His vicarious atonement for the sins of mankind by the shedding of His blood on the cross; the resurrection of His body from the tomb; His power to save men from sin; the new birth through the regeneration by the Holy Spirit; and the gift of eternal life by the grace of God.

This charter shall never be amended, modified, altered, or changed as to the provisions hereinbefore set forth.

THE INSPIRATION OF THE BIBLE, BOTH THE OLD AND THE NEW TESTAMENTS

The opening statement, *I believe in the inspiration of the Bible, both the Old and the New Testaments*, is all-important; indeed, upon its truth depends the truth of all the other statements. All we know about sin and salvation, heaven and hell, eternal life and death, the plan and purpose of God, and about His will for our lives is revealed in no other place than in the Word of God. Undermine faith in its infallibility, its authority, and its divine inspiration, and the whole house will crumble, because His Word is the foundation upon which all rests.

There are many theories about the inspiration of the Bible. Even in orthodox circles there are various shades of ideas on the subject. The increasing tendency is to disregard the old interpretation. According to the New Evangelicals (than whom there are no groups more dangerous), we need to "restudy" the question. But Bob Jones University does not agree with that idea. We think that all we need to do is to accept what God's Word says about the matter. Of course, if one does not believe that the Bible actually is God's Word, he has no foundation upon which to base his position.

In ordinary conversation, other things than the Bible are referred to as having been inspired. Sometimes a sermon is so described; and if it is a scriptural sermon, the term, in a sense, is well applied. Again, it is said that Shakespeare was inspired when he wrote a certain play; that Handel or some other musician was inspired when he composed certain music; that El Greco or another artist was inspired when he painted a particular picture. The term of reference of the word as used in these instances is that the author, the composer, or the painter must have had within himself when he created that word a sense of great urgency and drive—something above the normal and mortal grasp in art or music or literature.

But when we speak of inspiration as applied to the Word of God, we mean something quite different. This is a unique inspiration; it stands so far above all other inspiration as to be incomparable therewith. Literally, the word *inspired* means "God-breathed." It has root in a simple Latin word *inspirare*, which means "breathe into." Thus when we say that the Bible is the inspired Word of God, we mean that the book has breathed into it the very spirit and truth of an eternal God—that those who set down the sacred record were moved upon not by their own emotions, not by their own "soul quality," not by their own subject matter, but by the Holy Spirit of God Himself (II Peter 1:21).

Our belief in this doctrine goes still deeper: we believe in the *plenary* or full inspiration of the Word; i.e., that the book—all of it—is equally and fully inspired. Moreover, we subscribe to the *verbal* inspiration of Scripture, which is to say that in the original Hebrew manuscripts which the Old Testament writers wrote, and in the original Greek manuscripts which the New Testament writers wrote, God Himself chose the *very word* that should be put down to convey exactly what He meant to convey. This precludes any possibility of human personality intruding upon and interfering with what God had to say.

We do not mean to imply by this that God merely dictated the Word to those who wrote it—that He made out of them a typewriter upon which His fingers played. God does not intrude upon human personality in that way. He did more than dictate; His Holy Spirit moved upon men of different talents, different backgrounds, and different interests to set down in their own style His eternal truth. Some of these men were shepherds; some were scholars; some were peasants; and two of them were kings. Moses, the great lawgiver, was brilliant; he was a graduate of the University of Heliopolis, and "was learned in all the wisdom of the Egyptians" (Acts 7:22). Other writers were "unlearned and ignorant men" (Acts 4:13). Naturally the style of these men would be different. God did not go beyond the style of each. Never did He force upon a writer some word not already in his vocabulary. Instead, out of each man's talent, experience, and vocabulary, God chose the right word and illustration so that His truth might be preserved in the writing. Any man who does not believe in verbal inspiration is in danger of not believing in inspiration at all.

The difference in the writing style of each man is interesting. Paul, for instance, did not write in the same style as did James. Usually a speaker or writer discusses things in which he is deeply interested. Paul, though a Jew, had been reared in Tarsus, a Greek city. In his heritage were the Greek games, which were big events in Hellenic cities. Hence, we find not strange his frequent use of illustrations that had to do with athletic affairs. "Wherefore seeing we also are compassed about with so great a cloud of witnesses, let us lay aside every weight, and the sin which doth so easily beset us, and let us run with patience the race that is set before us" (Hebrews 12:1). "Know ye not that they which run in a race run all, but one receiveth the prize? So run, that ye may obtain" (I Corinthians 9:24; Galatians 2:2). "I press toward the mark for the prize of the high calling of God in Christ Jesus" (Philippians 3:14). "I have fought a good fight, I have finished my course, I have kept the faith" (II Timothy 4:7). James, on the other hand, though he, too, was a Jew, and though he dealt with many of the same subjects treated by Paul, had no background of Greek civilization; therefore his illustrations were different. Still, each of these men, out of his own experiences and vocabulary, was used of God to set down a portion of God's Word, which is forever settled in heaven (Psalm 119:89) and which He has magnified above all His Name (Psalm 138:2).

The same is true with regard to the Gospel writers. Though the personality of these men differed, God used words and terms natural to them, yet without allowing any error to creep in. Luke was a physician, and he wrote in the language of that profession. In his Gospel, we read of Christ's healing the woman with an issue of blood. A physician naturally would have noted that she "had spent all her living upon physicians, neither could be healed of any" (Luke 8:43). A physician could make such a comment without arousing the protests which such a statement from a layman would call forth. A true statement, God inspired Luke to set it down to give us an accurate picture of her situation.

But some may ask, "Do you mean that everything in the Bible is true?" No, we do not. There are lies in the Bible. There are half-truths in the Bible. Let me explain. In the Word the devil speaks; and what the devil says is usually a lie. God says that he is "a liar, and the father of it" (John 8:44). Almost everything the devil says, you can be sure, is a lie. Man speaks in the Bible, and what man says may or may not be true. But God speaks in this book, and where He speaks, *it is always the truth:* for God cannot lie (Titus 1:2). When we say that "whatever the Bible says is so" we mean that it is accurate in record. When it says the devil said something, he said it; and it is accurately recorded without being twisted, slanted, or warped.

It is possible to tell the truth in such a fashion as to make it a lie—to say something in a way that, insofar as the words are concerned, will be the absolute truth, yet will convey the wrong impression. That is the reason for the oath in court "to tell the truth, the whole truth, and nothing but the truth." The most satanic effort is the effort that uses a little truth and by using that little truth gives the wrong impression. Christian Science does that; it is a false religion because it takes a little truth and uses it to "sugar-coat" much poison. When someone speaks, he should speak fully and frankly and honestly to give the right impression. At a trial in court a stenographer with a little shorthand machine takes down everything that is said. The witness being examined may lie; but what he says goes into the record. Even though later it may be proven that the witness perjured himself, what is in the record is what he actually said. That is the way God keeps the record. Though the quote from the devil or from man may be a lie, God has it set down accurately; and God never makes an error.

There is one general principle to be applied to Bible study. When a man writes under divine inspiration, he "hangs the key" to the book near either the front door or the back door. By this I mean the key will be found near the beginning or toward the end of the book. In the book of Ecclesiastes, for example, the wise man says in the opening verses, "I have seen many things, and I have come to the conclusion that all is vanity."

There is much truth in the book of Ecclesiastes—a lot of good advice. One of the most beautiful passages in all the Word of God is, "Remember now thy Creator in the days of thy youth, while the evil days come not, nor the years draw nigh, when thou shalt say, I have no pleasure in them" (Ecclesiastes 12:1). Then, from that point the writer goes on to describe how old age comes. "Those that look out of the windows be darkened," meaning that older people begin to lose their sight. "The grinders cease because they are few"—most of their teeth are gone. "The golden bowl be broken"—mental power fails, memory leaves them. All of that is beautiful description, and it contains much truth. However, God did not give us the book of Ecclesiastes to teach us doctrine. Rather, He gave it to show how life looks to a wise, thoughtful man. It is a safe rule to beware of any religion that goes to this book for the text that proves its doctrine, for it is a false religion. To find doctrinal teaching, we must turn to the Epistles, whose purpose is to teach sound doctrine. Knowledge of history and prophecy is to be gleaned from certain books of the Old Testament. The life of Christ, of course, is recorded in the Gospels. All of these things have part in what God wanted set down for His children of all generations.

Someone has said, "Either this book will keep you from sin, or sin will keep you from this book." Sinners do not like to read the Bible because they find in it a picture of themselves; and it is never a good picture. Someone else has said, "I know this is God's Word. Only God could have written it. A bad man would not write it, because it shows man to be as bad as he is, and no man likes that picture of himself. A good man would not have written it, because it claims to be God's Word; and a good man would not lie about it. Therefore, only God could have written it. A bad man wouldn't; a good man wouldn't so God must have."

Young people, this book makes known God's plan, God's revelation of Himself, God's picture of man, and God's judgment that awaits the sin of man. It sets down the will of God for men, the plan of God for men, the message of God for men, and the method to be employed in presenting the message. This book is the very foundation of our faith. If it be not God's Word, then we might as well "close up shop" right now; for all our doctrine is found in this book.

Christian people may not always agree on how to interpret the Bible, but there are no contradictions therein. If you read something in the Bible that seems to contradict something else, you can be very sure of one of two things: either you do not understand the Word of God, or what you think is a contradiction is not a contradiction but a difference made in translation or something else. There are no contradictions in the Word of God, because God will not contradict Himself.

A man asked, "Don't you think James is in conflict with Paul? Paul taught, 'Ye are saved by faith . . . not of works' (Ephesians 2:8), whereas James taught, 'Faith, if it hath not works, is dead' " (James 2:17). There is no conflict between these two men. Remember Paul also said, "Work out your own salvation with fear and trembling" (Philippians 2:12).

To explain this to someone I asked, "Have you ever lived on a farm?"

"Yes," he replied, "I lived on a farm in West Virginia."

"Did you have a pump on the farm?" I asked.

"Yes," he said. "When I was a little boy, we installed a pump so that we would not have to go down the hill to the stream in the valley to get our water supply."

"Well," I continued, "did you ever have a real drought and have the pump go dry?"

"Yes," he answered. "One summer when I was about eighteen we had a big drought and everything dried up—including the pump."

"Did you try to pump?" I inquired.

"Yes, but all I got was air. There was no water."

Then I explained, "That is just what James and Paul are talking about. You are to work out your salvation with fear and trembling. Salvation is a gift of God; and you are to take the gift. Then, when you have it, it is your business to live the kind of life that will show men what you have. James tries to show that faith is proved—made perfect—by works."

Not all the writers always agreed personally, as men. The record says that Paul and Peter had a real disagreement at Antioch. They argued; and what they argued about is accurately recorded (Galatians 2). When Paul and Peter wrote the truths of God, however, they agreed, because they were writing under divine inspiration as God's Spirit brooded over them. So, God accurately preserved the words which were set down; and they say exactly what God meant to say.

When God finished the sacred record, His revelation to man was complete. Today God does not send dreams and visions to show man what He wants him to do. Visions and dreams were for the period before the record was complete. At that time God had to speak by the prophets. Since He completed what He wanted preserved, He has withheld special revelations. Since that time it has been His method to bring to life in the mind and heart and soul of a preacher a passage in His Word so that the preacher will stand up and proclaim the truth of God. Such a man has opportunity to predict and interpret trends, not because he is moved by the Spirit in the way that He moved upon the prophets of old, but because God has taken the revelation of His plan in the Word and made it real to the preacher so that he may proclaim it in and apply it to the present day. All man needs of the will of God is in the Word of God.

If ever you hear a man deliberately preach something that is contrary to the written Word, it matters not how eloquent that man may be, you may be sure he is not God's man. The man who does not have faith in the veracity of this book, divinely inspired of God, has no right to call himself a preacher of the truth; for the Word of God says that His Word is truth, and that it is to be hidden in the heart that we might not sin against God. The Bible is God's Word; and it is the only book that keeps man from sin.

It is fashionable nowadays to say, "I believe the Bible *contains* the Word of God." Beware of anyone who says that. The Bible does not merely *contain* the Word of God; it *is* the Word of God. There is a difference. To say that it contains the Word of God means that there may be parts of it that are not His Words. In such cases man sets his puny mind to decide what is and what is not truth, what is and what is not God's Word. He makes his mind judge the book, whereas the book is supposed to judge his thoughts. The person who does not believe in the inspiration of the Bible has no right to claim to be a Christian; for all we know of Christ and Christianity is revealed in this book, God's holy and inspired Word. When someone says that it only contains the Word of God, he is either untaught, or he is unsound in the faith. No Bible-believing Christian would make such a statement.

Some people claim that we worship the book. We do not. We worship the God Who wrote the book and the God Who is revealed in the book.

I do not have time to go into all of it, but it is interesting to note how many times the psalmist cries out in the 119th Psalm "According to thy word." "Quicken thou me (25, 154); strengthen thou me (28); uphold me (116); be merciful unto me (58); give me understanding (169); deliver me (170); Let thy mercies come also unto me, O Lord, even thy salvation (41); Thou hast dealt well with thy servant, O Lord" (65); and all of these "according to thy word." Then the psalmist exclaims, "How sweet are thy words unto my taste! yea, sweeter than honey to my mouth!" (119:103).

"The Word of God is quick, and powerful, and sharper than any twoedged sword, piercing even to the dividing asunder of soul and spirit, and of the joints and marrow, and is a discerner of the thoughts and intents of the heart" (Hebrews 4:12). All things are upheld "by the word of his power" (Hebrews 1:3). His Word is like a fire and like a hammer that breaks in pieces the rocks. "Therefore, behold, I am against the prophets, saith the Lord, that steal my words every one from his neighbour" (Jeremiah 23:29, 30).

"All scripture is given by inspiration of God, and is profitable for doctrine, for reproof, for correction, for instruction in righteousness: that the man of God may be perfect, throughly furnished unto all good works" (II Timothy 3:16). "Wherewithal shall a young man cleanse his way? by taking heed thereto according to thy word" (Psalm 119:9). If we did not have this blessed Word of God we would have no Christian faith. All we know about Jesus Christ, the author and finisher of our faith (Hebrews 12:2), is in the Word of God. How do we know that God gave men certain commandments by which to live? They are recorded in the book. How do we know that He is coming back again someday? The Word so declares it. This Word is the only body of truth in the world, complete, without error. The reason men hate it is that it is a restraint unto man, and that God in the book reveals Himself. They turn from it because they love darkness rather than light and because their deeds are evil (John 3:19). The holy and inspired Word of God is designed to be a lamp unto our feet, and a light unto our paths (Psalm 119:105). By it we are to judge all things.

Man tends to reverse things and judge the book by what he

sees. For instance, a man holds up the Bible; and as far as he goes in what he says, he preaches in line with what the Bible says. At the close of his message men begin to walk the aisles for salvation. Onlookers say, "That is good, I *saw* the preacher hold up the Bible and I *heard* him quote from it. This response is good; it is a result of the preaching of the Word." But wait a minute. What does the Word say about what you saw? How does the situation appear in its light? John said, "Whosoever transgresseth, and abideth not in the doctrine of Christ, hath not God. He that abideth in the doctrine of Christ, he hath both the Father and the Son. If there come any unto you, and bring not this doctrine, receive him not into your house, neither bid him God speed: For he that biddeth him God speed is partaker of his evil deeds" (II John 9-11). Go back now. What did you see in that meeting when so many men walked the aisles for salvation? Were there on the platform men who did not believe in the doctrines of Christ—His virgin birth, His vicarious atonement, His resurrection? Were they received by the preacher and perhaps invited to lead in prayer? God said, "Do not receive such men." Therefore, that evangelist, whoever he may be, disobeyed God. Did the evangelist send new converts into the churches of those who do not abide in the doctrines of Christ? If so, he bade them Godspeed—he helped the false teachers build congregations to listen to their erroneous teaching. All of this is in direct opposition to what God says; and we are without excuse if we "go along" in such unscriptural endeavors. God's Word clearly warns us with regard to separating ourselves from error in any guise. The Holy Spirit, writing through the Apostle Paul, said: "Be ye not unequally yoked together with unbelievers" (II Corinthians 6:14). "Withdraw yourselves from every brother that walketh . . . not after the tradition which he received of us" (II Thessalonians 3:6). "Mark them which cause divisions and offences contrary to the doctrine which ye have learned; and avoid them" (Romans 16:17). "If any man teach otherwise, and consent not to wholesome words, even the words of our Lord Jesus Christ, and to the doctrine which is according to godliness . . . from such withdraw thyself" (I Timothy 6:3-5). But you argue, "I saw the results." What does that prove? When Moses disobeyed God and smote the rock twice instead of speaking to it once as God had commanded, the water gushed forth, and the people had their thirst quenched.

Nevertheless, God punished Moses because he failed to believe Him and to sanctify Him in the eyes of the children of Israel (Numbers 20). God honors the disobedience of no man. Some fruit may result, but God's orchard is harmed for future fruit-bearing.

When God speaks, He always speaks the truth; and He expects man to act in accordance therewith. Paul wrote under divine inspiration; but when he stopped to discuss whether or not a man should be single or married, he explained, "I have no revelation on this point; I am putting it in as my opinion." Only a divinely inspired book would be that accurate.

The Bible is God-breathed. Different translations have been made, and in the translation a slight error may have crept in. This is a favorite argument of those who would discredit the book and cry out for the "modern" translations. But every word in the original manuscript was God-breathed. The men who undertook the translation of the King James Version were godly men who believed that they were handling God's holy and inspired Word, and therefore prayerfully undertook their task. But when the translators of the Revised Standard Version got together, only one man claimed to believe the Bible unequivocally. In view of scriptural teaching, this man violated Scripture when he became yoked together with infidels. Then, when this group translated in Isaiah, "Behold, a young girl shall conceive and bear a son," this man who knew that God meant virgin should have insisted that it be so included in the record; or he should have gotten off the committee and refused to let them use his name in connection with the translation. When a group of godly men who believe that this is God's Word join efforts, a fairly accurate translation results. On the other hand, when a group of modernists and unbelievers and scoffers get together to reword it in "modern" language, having in their midst only one man who believes in the inerrancy of the Scripture (and that man is disobeying God by sitting in the seat of the scornful), the result can never be in exact conformity to truth. I will trust the translation made by godly men who know they are dealing with God's Word rather than the translation of a group of worldly-wise scholars who look upon the Bible as simply another book of religion and story and poetry to be translated and thereby handle it deceitfully.

The godly man, the Scripture says, delights in the law of the Lord, and meditates therein day and night (Psalm 1:2).

As with the prophet (Jeremiah 15:16), so should it be with us that His Word shall be the joy and rejoicing of our hearts. We should approach it with reverential awe. The old Jew, when he was handed the scroll to read, used to kiss the Scripture before he gave it back to the Rabbi. It might not be a bad habit for a Christian today when reading the book at night to kiss the sacred page. All down the ages it has been a light to the path of man and revelation of the truth and love of God. "Search the scripture," commands our Lord. "Receive it with readiness of mind," says the Apostle Paul (Acts 17:11). "Speak of it," urges the psalmist (Psalm 119:172). This is a wonderful book. Let us feed upon it; believe it; trust it; obey it.

THE CREATION OF MAN BY THE DIRECT ACT OF GOD

In our last lesson we discussed the most important phrase of our Creed—*the inspiration of the Bible, both the Old and the New Testaments.* The foregoing statement cannot be overemphasized, for upon its truth hinges all our theology. Our faith is built upon the promises of God which are revealed in His Word; and if we cannot depend upon it as infallible, authoritative, and divinely inspired, we have no assurance of anything. We sing "On Christ, the solid Rock I stand; All other ground is sinking sand"; and that is true. However, the Christ upon Whom we stand is *the Christ of the Word.* In a real sense, therefore, this book underlies and undergirds all our beliefs.

The second statement of our Creed is *the creation of man by the direct act of God.* I am not a scientist, and I shall not attempt to speak scientifically. That is a good policy for all of you—especially you young preachers. Nothing is more ridiculous than for a person of limited knowledge in science to try to use the jargon of science. Even though the preacher may possess scientific knowledge, those who listen may not; therefore, the most effective plan is to come down to plain facts in simple language so that all may understand.

God's Word was not given to us to teach us science. Nevertheless, the same God Who wrote the book made the laws which govern science; and He would not cause to be set down in His Word anything that would be contrary to His own laws. Thus when we read in Genesis "God created man" (1:27), we must accept it as a fact.

Evolution teaches that man was not created by a single and direct act of God but that he evolved from lower forms of life. There are many theories of evolution—almost as many theories as there are evolutionists. All are in fact based to some degree, however, upon the "Darwinian Theory." Charles Darwin was a British naturalist who lived in the 19th century. He traveled around the world observing primitive forms of life—both animal and vegetable. In the South Pacific, he made a study of life forms not seen in his native Britain. Eventually he began to speculate that life possibly came from one source—that is, that all forms of life as we know them today had origin in one cell, one primitive form of life. Darwin summarized his speculations and had them published in a book which he called *The Origin of Species*. In this book Darwin does not make the blunt claim that anything evolved from some other form of life. Instead, he prefaces his remarks with "we may assume," "we may conclude," "we may suppose," "it seems likely," or some other inconclusive phrase. His was mere supposition, but out of it atheistic scientists built a system which the devil has used to destroy man's faith in the Word of God. On his deathbed Darwin expressed regret that the book he had intended to be nothing more than a sort of speculation had been used to weaken man's belief in God's Word.

The general idea of the evolutionary theories is this: In the warm seas thousands and thousands of years ago one cell of life existed. As the ages went by, this cell developed in various directions. Single cells began to expand and divide: one cell became two cells, which in turn divided into four, and so on. By and by, two or three cells decided to stick together—in unity there was strength. How they reasoned it out, I do not know; but in some way they agreed to hang together instead of "hanging separately." They had a sort of congress of single cells and voted to unite to become some kind of fish—a slightly higher form of life. Remember, none of this happened overnight. Millions of years may have elapsed between stages of development. One day when the sun was shining on one part of the creature, it decided that that would be a good place to grow an eye; so certain of the cells volunteered to be an eye. After another period of a few million years, one of these creatures decided that it might be interesting to see what was on land. In order to do this, it would need lungs with which to breathe air; and it developed lungs. On the land it slithered and slid; but finding this to be uncomfortable and slow, certain cells decided to protrude themselves to form appendages upon which to move. From these appendages, after about another million years, legs developed and the creature began to walk. As it walked around, it looked upward and started admiring the beautiful things in the sky. To further adapt themselves, some of the creatures grew wings, became birds, and flew away. Others chose to crawl around in the swamps as lizards. Still others found it hard to make a choice; so they developed both wings and tails to become flying lizards. By this process of adapting to an environment, man finally evolved. This is when trouble began: man took over.

You say, "Dr. Bob, you make this sound mighty ridiculous!"

That is what I am trying to do. To me, there is nothing more lacking in good sense than this evolutionary fiction. How any intelligent scientist can believe it amazes me; and contrary to general opinion, not *all* scientists believe in evolution. Some of the greatest scientists disclaim any belief therein. In Bob Jones University there are well-trained men of science; and none of these believe in evolution. If they did, we would not retain them to teach our young people, whose faith in God's Word we are seeking to strengthen, not destroy.

It is tragic how many schools which once held to the truth of God's Word now subscribe to what is popularly called theistic evolution. Within recent years, for example, a well-known independent and formerly orthodox school had on its campus a symposium for the discussion of science and the Bible and the history of beginnings. Without exception, the speakers favored evolution. The only protest came from a member of the Bible faculty who rose to question the trend of the conference, and he was laughed to scorn.

Those who sneeringly say of Bob Jones University, "It is always so contentious!" can notice in the tragic incident I just mentioned the end-result of failure to fight for the faith—A BREAKDOWN OF FAITH! If we do not contend for the faith, we will not keep the faith. Should Bob Jones University ever cease to have the kind of emphasis presently maintained in the daily chapel programs, we will go the way most other schools have gone. It is impossible to keep a school true to God's Word without proclaiming and fighting for what you believe. The same is true in the individual life. If you do not fight to give your testimony—to make known where you stand with regard to God's Word—you will find that your faith becomes less important to you. Contending for the faith is essential; that is why God commands it (Jude 3).

What is the theistic view of evolution embraced by many in so-called Christian schools and pulpits? The word *theistic* means "taking God into account." A theistic evolutionist, then, is one who says, "I believe that God was in all of this—that He brought man into being by a process of evolution." In other words, he attempts to reconcile Genesis to evolution. But it cannot be done; the two are irreconcilable. No matter who he may be and no matter what he may claim, no evolutionist believes the Word of God. He may be a deist—believe in some sort of god—but he has no right to call himself a Christian, because he disbelieves God's record.

Everything in creation was prepared for man. God set the stage and then took counsel, as a Trinity, and said: "Let us make man in our image, after our likeness." Then the sacred record adds, "So God created man in his own image, in the image of God created he him, male and female created he them." Speaking further of the creation of woman, it says, "And the Lord God caused a deep sleep to fall upon Adam, and he slept: and he took one of his ribs, and closed up the flesh thereof; and the rib, which the Lord God had taken from man, made he a woman." Man and woman were to be of one flesh. Certainly that would disprove "theistic evolution." According to Genesis, woman could not have "evolved" along with man; by a direct act of God she was made from the rib of the man who had already been created by a direct act of God. Man was made first because in the economy of God he is to be lord over the woman.

Throughout the Word of God is indicated the fact that God deals with man as man and woman. The type of Christ and His Church is the union of man and wife: the man is head of the wife as Christ is Head of the Church. Much of the trouble in the world revolves around the reversal of God's plan of headship which He vested in the man. Woman was created to be "an help meet for him." She was made out of man's rib to be subject to him; and the rib was near his heart so that she might be loved by him.

If God made woman from man (and He did!), it had to be an instantaneous act. It would have been impossible to have spread out over millions of years the process of woman "evolving" from a rib. Moreover, man all this time would have been mating with some other low creature like himself, for evolution admits that at this point creatures had already divided into male and female, that reproduction had become sexual in the "advanced" forms of life, and that some sort of offspring had resulted therefrom. But God, in His Word, declares that man was created "fully developed" from the beginning. Indeed, he was placed in the Garden of Eden to dress and to keep it; and he "gave names to all cattles ... fowl of the air, and to every beast of the field." Woman also was created "fully developed" and was brought "unto the man." The creation of man was literally an instantaneous act on the part of God and hence is irreconcilable with any evolutionary process.

But suppose man did evolve from some lower form of life; where along the line did he become an immortal being? The record states that "God formed man of the dust of the ground, and breathed into his nostrils the breath of life; and man became a living soul" (2:7). It does not say that he became a living *creature*. No other creature of earth is described as having a soul. Man alone has hope of immortality. Let a cow fall dead in the pasture, and all the other cows will continue to graze as though nothing had happened. They will show no concern for the dead cow. Though an animal, by natural instinct of self-preservation, may be frightened by the attack of some natural enemy and try to protect itself, there is in it no dread of death such as is inherent in man. I am sure no animal ever speculates on what lies beyond death; when a beast dies, it goes back to dust and that is the end of it. With man, however, it is different: he must live somewhere forever. Man is an immortal being, and his immortal soul did not develop through any evolutionary hypothesis. God breathed His own breath into him.

A man with whom I was trying to discuss the destiny of his

soul said to me, "I do not believe man has a soul. I am an evolutionist. I do not accept the Genesis account of creation."

"Did you ever read Genesis?" I asked.

"No," he answered; "I never did."

"Let me read it to you," I said; and I took out my Bible and read the account of creation.

When I had finished, he said to me: "One thing I will have to admit. That is a lot more simple and clear than most evolutionary theories. I wish I could believe it."

There are many questions we cannot answer with regard to the creation of man. But one thing is certain: he did not evolve. God tells us all He wants us to know; and this He expects us to accept by faith. Beyond what is written, we are not to speculate.

Within the different species there is development. For instance, people in our day are taller than people of the 12th and 13th centuries. It is easy to observe this by noticing the armor which was worn by knights of the earlier period—it looks like children's armor. Every succeeding generation is somewhat taller than the one before. That, however, is not evolution. No matter what elements of similarity may exist in different forms of life, they are no proof of evolution. Each structure serves its purpose. If a certain form of life or development for a certain purpose satisfies God, He makes it so.

The whole theory of evolution is foolish. Never be disturbed or bothered by it. Compare the guesses of men with the facts of God's Word, and you will easily see the superiority of the biblical record. Bob Jones University believes that man was created in the image of God by a direct act, even as God said. There is no room in our Creed for an evolutionary theory.

The process of the human race has not been upward from the swamp by evolution, but downward from the garden by sin. In a perfect environment man sinned; and the result of that sin is apparent in the world today. Every generation of mankind, instead of being better, has been basically worse for the reason that it has been another generation of sin and flight from God. With modern improvement of food and drugs, the physical span of man's life has been extended. But as far as his spiritual and moral conditions are concerned, he is going downward; and in our generation he has sunk about as low as he can go on earth. He has messed up his government; he faces problems that are beyond his power to solve; he has discovered scientific means of destruction that he is afraid to handle; his heart is failing him for fear of those things which shall come upon the earth; moral conditions are deplorable. Apart from God, that has ever been the course of man, though he does not like to admit it. Sinful man likes to think that he is master of his environment, that he is a creature of great gifts and talents, that he has no need of God, nor indeed of anything. But that is not true. God's Word says that it is in Him that "we live, and move, and have our being" (Acts 17:28).

The evolutionary theory completely sets at naught John 3:16. The Bible says, "God is love." God created man as an act of love so that man could fellowship with Him. However, He gave to man a free will to *choose* to love Him. But man sinned and caused his fellowship with God to be broken. The saddest cry of the Old Testament is God's cry in the garden, "Adam, where art thou?" What a picture! Man who had been created to love God and to fellowship with Him trying to hide behind the trees which God had placed there for man's food! And what love! God seeking out to redeem from his sinful state the man who had deliberately disobeyed Him! Evolution is the opposite of this picture. It has in it no hint of love. It is a cruel process of the "survival of the fittest," which means that the form of life that could not satisfactorily adapt to its environment could not live. The creature that came out of the sea, if it could not develop lungs or could not work out some means to feed and protect itself, would die. In other words, "the fit survive, and the unfit die."

Why any man would choose to believe in such a cold, cruel process rather than in the warmth of God's loving care and tender mercy is beyond me. The Bible says of them, "Professing themselves to be wise, they became fools" (Romans 1:22).

If you will study your history, you will find that about 100 years ago or a little more, certain things began to develop simultaneously in modern life that have hastened the breaking down of respect for God's law. These are the communistic theory of government, the evolutionary theory of origin, and the growing emphasis upon the central authority and infallibility of the pope in Roman Catholicism. Satan, knowing that his time is short, began to double his attack upon the citadel of faith by using all of these elements—the growing power of the Vatican, the growing force of Communism, and the breakdown of faith through evolutionary hypotheses. These belong together as equally satanic and equally dangerous.

Man, though he was created in the image of God, fell from the place where God meant him to be; and he has need of God's regenerating grace to restore him. May God help us to abide in His true doctrines and not be "carried about with every wind of doctrine, by the sleight of men, and cunning craftiness, whereby they lie in wait to deceive" (Ephesians 4:14).

THE INCARNATION AND VIRGIN BIRTH OF OUR LORD AND SAVIOUR, JESUS CHRIST

We come now to the person and work of our Lord—first, *the incarnation and virgin birth of our Lord and Saviour, Jesus Christ.* A Christian is one who believes God; and God makes it clear in His Word that His Son is God in the flesh (I Timothy 3:16) and that he was born of a virgin.

The word *incarnate* is derived from simple Latin meaning "in flesh." The English word *carnal* cames from the same root. A carnal Christian is one who "lives after the flesh." Another word which stems from this root is *carnival.* Although we usually associate it with a side show or merry-go-round, the original meaning is a "farewell-to-the-flesh" celebration which preceded Lent, a 40-day period of fasting and penitence which some liturgical churches observe. In countries where they make much of Lent—particularly in strong Roman Catholic countries—there is, during the three days immediately preceding this season, a carnival—a time of dissipation supposed to be a last "binge" before saying a farewell to the flesh for 40 days. To say farewell to the flesh, they attend masked balls where they drink, carouse, and engage in sin.

Incarnation means "in the flesh." Applied to the Lord Jesus Christ, the term means "God embodied in flesh"—"Immanuel . . . God with us" (Isaiah 7:14; Matthew 1:23). The Bible explicitly teaches that the God of the Ages, "the Lamb slain from the foundation of the world" (Revelation 13:8), took upon Himself the flesh and form of man and walked upon this earth as a man. In Philippians 2:8, He is described as "being found in fashion as a man." The One Who is "the same yesterday, today, and for ever" (Hebrews 13:8), became "flesh and dwelt among us" (John 1:14); and in Him dwelled "all the fulness of the Godhead bodily" (Colossians 2:9).

One of the heresies of the early church was that Jesus Christ came into being when He was born of Mary. That is not true. Jesus Christ is as eternal as God is eternal, for *He is God.* John emphasizes this. "In the beginning," he says, "was the Word, and the Word was with God, and the Word was God" (John 1:1). Then he repeats, "The same was *in the beginning* with God." Jesus Himself taught His eternality and oneness with the Father: "Before Abraham was, I am" (John 8:58); "I and my Father are one" (John 10:30); "My Father worketh hitherto, and I work. Therefore the Jews sought to kill him, because he not only had broken the sabbath, but said also that God was his Father, making himself equal with God" (John 5:17-18).

Jesus Christ made many appearances to earth before His birth in Bethlehem. The Angel of the Covenant, the Angel of the Lord, and similar appellations of the Old Testament have reference to the Lord Jesus Christ in pre-incarnate appearances. We tend to think of angels as winged creatures. God's Word so describes the cherubim and seraphim (Isaiah 6:2; Ezekiel 1:6), but there is no scriptural basis for such a description of angels. We do not know what an angel looks like. As long as we are in the flesh, if we see one (and we may!), we will see a person; for to men, an angel looks like a man.

In the plains of Mamre Abraham saw three men standing before him (Genesis 18). Though they looked like men, they were angels—one of them the Angel of the Covenant, the Lord Himself. When two of the angels went on to Sodom to pluck Lot and his family from the doomed city, the Angel of the Covenant remained with Abraham. There are places where God will not go, things God cannot do, and people with whom God does not associate. If a man backslides, God may deal with Him; but He will not fellowship with him in his backslidden state. How much better it is to have God dwell in our home and fellowship with us than to have Him merely send angels to pluck us out of dangers that come from sin. If we do not obey God and are not in fellowship with Him, we cannot find His presence close at hand. He will deal with us—will chastise and discipline us—but fellowship with Him demands *obedience*.

At Peniel Jacob wrestled all night with "a man"; and this Man was Jesus Christ (Genesis 32:24-32). At Jericho a Man with a drawn sword stood in front of Joshua; "and Joshua . . . said unto him, Art thou for us, or for our adversaries?" (Joshua 5:13-15). The Man with the sword replied, "As captain of the host of the Lord am I now come." Then "Joshua fell on his face to the earth, and did worship," for this Captain of the Lord's host was Jesus Christ.

But when He came to earth to pay the price of man's sin and so make him acceptable to a sinless God, the Son of God had to come, not in the appearance of man as in Old Testament times, but actually as a man in human flesh. He had to do more than *look* like man—*He had to be man!* The reason for this is simple: Man, in the flesh, sinned. The carnal nature—that is, the fleshly nature—of man *is* sinful and must be punished. "For to be carnally minded is death" (Romans 8:6). Thus, in order to take upon Him the sin of man and the penalty of man's sin, God took upon Himself the body of a man so that He might redeem man who, through sin, had sold himself under judgment. The blood of bulls and goats could not avail for sin, there being in those sacrifices "remembrance again made of sins every year" (Hebrews 10:3); therefore, Christ, once for all, appeared to put away sin by the sacrifice of Himself (Hebrews 9:26). He Who had *made* the first Adam *became* the Second Adam; and as in the first Adam all die, even so in the Second Adam shall all be made alive (I Corinthians 15:22). "As by one man's disobedience many were made sinners, so by the obedience of one shall many be made righteous" (Romans 5:19).

In His earthly body Jesus Christ was heir to all the sufferings that are attendant upon the mortal body. There was, however, this difference: in Him was no tendency to sin. He "was in all points tempted like as we are, yet without sin" (Hebrews 4:15). In the weakness of physical hunger and exhaustion He was tempted of the devil to "take a short cut" instead of following God's will. But He resisted the tempter and humbled Himself to the obedience of the Cross—the hour for which He had been born. Today the temptation to substitute "the short cut" for God's way plagues us. But in that He Himself has suffered being tempted, He is able to succor us when we are tempted (Hebrews 2:17, 18); and we do not have to yield to the devil's subtlety.

Until you understand the truth of the Incarnation, you will not find the treasures of God opened to you. It is like a chest which has two strong locks; before you can open the chest and revel in its treasures, you must have and use the key to both locks. So it is with the truth of the nature of our blessed Lord: there is both deity and humanity; and without both keys, one can never open the treasure chest. He is very God and at the same time very man.

Essential to, and inseparable from, the incarnation is

The Virgin Birth

For a man to say that he believes in the one and not in the other is to state an impossible thing. Indeed, the one presupposes the other. Had Jesus Christ been born of human parentage as other men are born, He would have fallen heir to sin as all generations since Adam and Eve sinned have been children of sin—have had in their bodies the seed of sin. But though Jesus Christ was born of woman as other men are, His birth was a supernatural miracle also; for there was no earthly father. "The birth of Jesus Christ was on this wise: When as his mother Mary was espoused to Joseph, before they came together, she was found with child of the Holy Ghost." The angel of the Lord appeared unto Joseph in a dream, and said to him, "Fear not to take unto thee Mary thy wife; for that which is conceived in her is of the Holy Ghost. . . . Then Joseph . . . took unto him his wife: And knew her not till she had brought forth her firstborn son: and he called his name JESUS" (Matthew 1:18-26).

Romanism teaches that Mary was conceived without sin and was sinless all of her life. The pope, who declared the sinlessness of Mary a doctrine of the Roman Church, was as fallible as all other men and nowhere shows more clearly how un-biblical Roman Catholic doctrine can be than in this case. Mary was one of the choice women of all time. She was "highly favoured" of the Lord and "blessed . . . among women" (Luke 1:28, 30). What an honor for her to be chosen to be the mother of the Son of God! Notice, however, that I said the mother of the Son of God and not the "Mother of God." Mary is the mother of the body of the Lord Jesus Christ. Hers was the womb that cradled the Holy One begotten of the Holy Spirit. She was a virtuous, fine, godly woman. Nevertheless, Mary was born in sin just as all men since the Fall have been born in sin; and she stood in need of a Saviour as do all men. God's Word says, "All have sinned, and come short of the glory of God" (Romans 3:23); "There is none righteous, no, not one" (Romans 3:10). It does not say, "All, but Mary, have sinned"; "None, but Mary, is righteous." As with all others, so with Mary: "Ye must be born again" (John 3:7). That Mary knew this is evidenced in the phrase of her song, "My spirit hath rejoiced in God *my* Saviour" (Luke 1:47). God chose Mary because she was a woman of faith. She believed "even as Abraham believed God, and it was accounted to him for righteousness" (Galatians 3:6). When Jesus Christ died on the Cross, He died for His mother after the flesh as He died for all men and women.

Tradition says that Mary was reading Isaiah's prophecy, "Behold, a virgin shall conceive, and bear a Son, and shall call his name Immanuel" (7:14), when the angel Gabriel appeared to her and announced that she would conceive in her womb, and bring forth a son, Whose Name shall be called JESUS. Whether or not this is true, no man can say. It is possible, however, for there is no doubt that a godly Jewish maiden such as Mary was well-versed in Messianic prophecy.

Someone once asked William Jennings Bryan, "Why do you emphasize the virgin birth? It is mentioned twice in the Bible."

The great statesman aptly replied, "How many times does God have to tell us something before we believe it? If He mentions something only once in His Word, that is all a person needs to know it is a fact."

Twice in God's Word—once in the Old Testament (Isaiah 7:14) and once in the New Testament (Matthew 1:23)—the virgin birth is clearly stated. But the doctrine is implied many times. Genesis 3:15, for example, refers to "the seed of the woman" bruising the serpent's head. Where in scientific literature is the seed spoken of as being in the woman? In the natural order of things, the seed is in the man; yet Moses, under divine inspiration, wrote of the promise of a virgin-born Redeemer. From this passage on through the Word of God we find this a dominant theme.

Why does it take so much faith to believe in the virgin birth? To quote Mr. Bryan again, "The birth of Christ is no more remarkable than the birth of any one of us. It is simply different. He Who gives life can give it any form that pleases Him." One of the great wonders of God's universe is the miracle of birth; and the God Who can bring to pass that miracle can bring His Son into the world by a special miracle of the virgin birth.

Jesus Christ, after the flesh, was a member of the Jewish race—the seed of David (Romans 1:3), a child of Abraham (Hebrews 2:16). He fulfilled the divine promise to the patriarch, "In thee shall all families of the earth be blessed" (Genesis 12:3). I cannot understand how a Christian could be caught in the anti-Semitism that prevails in so many places. Born-again Christians ought to love the Jew, for out of this race came our Saviour. Something is wrong with the Christian experience of one who does not have in his heart some love for these chosen ones of God and does not desire their salvation. On Israel now is a curse which dates back to the time when they rejected their Messiah and cried, "His blood be on us, and on our children" (Matthew 27:25). No race ever has been so persecuted and mistreated. The great proof of the Bible, somebody has said, is the fact that the Jews are still in the world. They have lived in all the nations of the earth—have been captives in all kingdoms—yet their identity is still apparent. Wonderful race! As Jonah in the body of the whale was not digested, so in the sea of nations the Jews have not been digested. God has preserved them, and they have been a blessing wherever they have lived. The nations that have turned against the Jews have gone down. In the 15th century, about the time that Columbus discovered America, Spain turned against the Jews; and she, who once was the most prosperous nation of Europe, now is the most wretched country in Western Europe. Miserable, dirty, depraved, backward, all her glory is departed. Hitler's notorious crimes against the Jews and the conditions that resulted therefrom are well-known. Nobody who has ever laid his hand against this people of God has prospered. The divine promise—"I will bless them that bless thee, and curse him that curseth thee" (Genesis 12:3)—still holds. Believers are commanded to pray for the peace of Jerusalem. There is blessing for those who do it.

"When the fulness of the time was come," says God's Word, "God sent forth his Son, made of a woman" (Galatians 4:4). Christ's being born of a virgin is essential, or else God is a liar; and "God is not a man, that he should lie" (Numbers 23:19). "He is a God of truth and without iniquity" (Deuteronomy 32:4). It is "impossible for him to lie" (Hebrews 6:18). If Jesus Christ be not virgin-born, He fails to meet the conditions that God said His Son would meet as to the manner in which He should come into the world. The virgin birth is essential to the deity of Christ. Moreover, it is as much an essential part of salvation as is the death of Jesus Christ on the Cross. Some men teach that it is possible to be a Christian without believing in the virgin birth. It is not. A man, when he comes to trust Christ as his personal Saviour, may not know what the Bible says about the virgin birth; but when he trusts Christ, he will not doubt any miracle of the Word. Whoever questions the miracles of God's Word has not experienced the miracle of regeneration. Only the virgin-born Son of God has power by His death and resurrection to save sinners. He "was delivered for our offences, and was raised again for our justification" (Romans 4:25), but we will discuss that in a later lesson. To disbelieve the virgin birth is to disbelieve the Christ Who has power to forgive sins; for if He be not born of a virgin, His death has no value for the forgiveness of sin.

HIS IDENTIFICATION AS THE SON OF GOD

H*is identification as the Son of God* is supported in Scripture by many incontrovertible testimonies. "Thou art the Christ, the Son of the living God," said Peter in answer to the Lord's question as to His identity (Matthew 16:16). "This is my beloved Son, in whom I am well pleased," declared the Voice from heaven at His baptism (Matthew 3:17) and again at the Transfiguration (Matthew 17:5). "Of a truth thou art the Son of God," confessed the disciples who saw Him still the troubled waves of a stormy sea (Matthew 14:33). "That holy thing which shall be born of thee shall be called the Son of God," announced the angel Gabriel to Mary (Luke 1:35). "I saw, and bare record that this is the Son of God," testified John the Baptist (John 1:34). Many others—John the beloved disciple (John 3:16-18); a man born blind, whose sight was restored by a miracle of Jesus (John 9:35-38); Martha, in whose home He visited (John 11:27); Mark (1:1) and Paul the great Apostle (Acts 9:20)—also testified to His divine Sonship. Even the powers of darkness recognized and obeyed Him. Demons said to Him, "What have we to do with thee, Jesus, thou Son of God? Art thou come hither to torment us before the time?" (Matthew 8:29). "The Father sent the Son to be the Saviour of the world," wrote John (I John 4:14, 15). "Whosoever shall confess that Jesus is the Son of God, God dwelleth in him, and he in God."

In one sense the Bible teaches that all men are children of God—not in the family sense, but in the sense that God made all mankind. Somewhat to the degree that the watchmaker is the father of the watch, God is the Father of all mankind. There is this difference, however. He made us, and He also created us; He made the elements out of which He made us. But in the family sense, God is the Father of only those who believe on Him Whom He hath sent. "As many as received him [that is, Jesus], to them gave he power to become the sons of God, even to them that believe on his name" (John 1:12). God is the Father, and Jesus Christ is the elder Brother, of all who have put their trust in the only begotten Son of God.

No man ever becomes a child of God until first he realizes that he is not a child of God, but a sinner. There are only two kinds of folk in the world—the children of God, and the children of Satan. "That which is born of the flesh is flesh; and that which is born of the Spirit is spirit. Marvel not that I said unto thee, Ye must be born again," said our Lord to Nicodemus (John 3:6, 7). Satan is the god of this world and the lord of the flesh. Jesus told the unbelieving Jews who claimed Abraham as their father "Ye are Abraham's seed . . . but . . . ye are of your father the devil" (John 8:37-44). By this He meant that if they were true children of Abraham—that is, spiritual children of the covenant, those who had entered into the spiritual heritage—they would recognize Him and reverence His Word instead of seeking to kill Him. He who does not recognize Jesus Christ as Saviour and reverence Him as Lord is a child of the devil. All men are either saints or sinners, children of God, or children of the devil; there is no middle ground.

Had you stopped to think that you are a saint? A man does not have to die and have some church council declare him a saint; he becomes a saint when he dies unto sin and becomes alive unto Christ. The moment you were born again, you became a saint. If you are not a saint, then you are not a child of God, but a sinner, and hence a child of the devil. Every man is in bondage to one of two forces—the force of sin, or the force of light. Either Christ is your Master, or Satan is your lord. The Bible makes it very clear that "No man can serve two masters: for either he will hate the one, and love the other; or else he will hold to the one, and despise the other"

(Matthew 6:24).

When you were born again, you became a child of God. However, you are not a begotten child of God. Jesus Christ is the "only begotten" of the Father (John 3:16). We are *born* of the Spirit; He was *begotten* of the Spirit. When we speak of "His identification as the Son of God," we mean something entirely different from what we mean about the rest of mankind—even about those who have been saved. His was indeed a unique Sonship.

"Liberalism" teaches that Jesus Christ simply realized His divinity and Sonship, and that all we need to do is recognize our sonship and try to live as a child of God. That is false doctrine. Jesus Christ did not just *realize* His divinity and Sonship. He *knew* Who He was. "I and my Father are one," He emphatically stated. He knew He was DEITY. He is the One Who from the beginning was with God (John 1:1-3), who claimed to be God (John 10:30), and who "thought it not robbery to be equal with God" (Philippians 2:6). Some men say, "I think He was just a good man. I do not believe that He was God in any special sense." If He is not God, He is not a good man, but one of the worst frauds who ever lived. He claimed to be God; and any man who is not what he claims to be is a liar. If Jesus Christ is not, in truth, the Son of God, none of us are, and never can be, children of God; for our sonship of the Father depends upon His being the unique Son of God.

Beware of men who speak of the divinity of Jesus. Whoever uses that terminology is either a modernist, or one who has come under the influence of modernistic books. The correct phrase is "the deity of Christ." There is a difference. He is not just divine; "He is very God of very God, One with God, co-eternal with the Father."

The body that died on the Cross was a human body, yet it was the body wherein Deity was incarnated. God dwelt in that flesh. In Heaven today, Jesus Christ has a human body. It is a body that was without sin, but which became sin for us and on the Cross of Calvary paid the penalty of our sin. This virgin-born Son of God in the flesh is our only hope of salvation and our great assurance of glorification. The fact that there is a body in Heaven is all the proof we need that someday we, too, will have a body in heaven. Our vile bodies will be changed like unto His glorious body (Philippians 3:21), "And so shall we ever be with the Lord" (I Thessalonians 4:17).

"We know that the Son of God is come, and hath given us an understanding, that we may know him that is true, and we are in him that is true, even in His Son Jesus Christ. This is the true God, and eternal life" (I John 5:20).

Never let anyone shake your faith in these great essentials. God's Word speaks; and where God speaks, let all men be liars. You stand with God and upon God's Word.

HIS VICARIOUS ATONEMENT FOR THE SINS OF MANKIND BY THE SHEDDING OF HIS BLOOD ON THE CROSS

Vicarious means "in the place of another" or "identifying oneself with another." Some people have a vicarious reaction while reading a book—that is, they tend to identify themselves with the characters in the book. When we speak of a vicarious atonement, however, there is a much deeper meaning. We mean that the Lord Jesus Christ on the Cross identified Himself with us; literally He took our place; He identified Himself with our sins. He suffered our penalty. He who knew no sin became sin for us "that we might be made the righteousness of God in him" (II Corinthians 5:21). In our behalf, in our stead, in our place, God's only begotten Son "bare our sins in his own body on the tree" (I Peter 2:24). He identified Himself with the criminal in order to take the criminal's penalty. He, by the grace of God, tasted death for every man (Hebrews 2:9); and when we accept Him as our personal Saviour, realizing that "He was wounded for our transgressions," that "he was bruised for our iniquities," that "the chastisement of our peace was upon him," and that "with his stripes we are healed" (Isaiah 53:5), we are identified with Him in righteousness.

The word *atonement* has somewhat the same meaning as propitiation. Jesus Christ "is the propitiation for our sins: and not for ours only, but also for the sins of the whole world" (I John 2:2). "Herein is love," we are told, "not that we loved God, but that he loved us, and sent his Son to be the propitiation for our sins" (I John 4:10). "All have sinned, and come short of the glory of God; Being justified freely by his grace through the redemption that is in Christ Jesus: Whom God hath set forth to be a propitiation through faith in his blood, to declare his righteousness for the remission of sins that are past, through the forbearance of God" (Romans 3:23-25). Pagans try to propitiate their gods by offerings and sacrifices. Let the storm rage, the wind blow, the tempest howl, and the pagan will make an offering or sacrifice in hopes of turning aside the anger of his god. The sacrifice may be a chicken, a coconut, or, in some countries, a child—but it is an attempt to make the god forget his wrath. A propitiation, then, is an offering or some act of humility by which an attempt is made to turn aside wrath, anger, indignation.

Atonement, though in a sense similar to propitiation, is slightly different in meaning. It means "reconciliation between two parties who had been separated by a difference." Broken down into its simplest form, it means *at-one-ment.* Two people are divided. Something happens which makes it possible for them to become one again in sympathy and understanding. Suppose you owe money to, or have damaged the property of, someone; and relations with that person have been broken. Then suppose someone else comes along and pays the money or damages, and you accept what he has done on your behalf. That person has reconciled you and your neighbor. By his action, the offense has been removed; and you and your neighbor are in accord again. That is what Jesus Christ did on the Cross for sinful man. "God was in Christ, reconciling the world unto himself" (II Corinthians 5:19).

As sinners, we were at enmity with God. We had wronged Him, and God could not look on us, could not fellowship with us, in that sinful state. But through the death of Jesus Christ on the Cross, that enmity was healed (Ephesians 2:16). The inspired writer expresses it, "For he is our peace, who hath made both one, and hath broken down the middle wall of partition between us" (Ephesians 2:14); and we are able to come "boldly unto the throne of grace, that we may obtain mercy, and find grace to help in time of need" (Hebrews 4:16).

In other words, between God and us was the wall of our sins. God could not tolerate sin; so we were separated from God. But when Jesus Christ paid the price of sin—suffered for sin—our sins were put away; and by faith in His finished work we become sinless in God's sight. The wall of partition is broken down, God's anger is turned aside—not because He forgets to be angry, but because His wrath against sin is satisfied by the death of His Son, Who was the perfect Sacrifice.

The Bible speaks of God's being "just, and the justifier of him which believeth in Jesus" (Romans 3:26). Because God is God, there are certain things He cannot do. He cannot overlook, cannot simply forget, sin. He Who is just must be absolutely fair in every little act and aspect of His law. His very justice demands His judgment. Justice demands that the law be obeyed or the penalty exacted. A good judge would not set aside the law even for his own son. In our system a judge ordinarily would not be permitted to act if he were biased in relationship to any of the people on trial. But suppose such a case did exist, and a son were on trial before his father as the judge. Suppose the jury found him guilty. As a father, the judge would love his child; but as the judge, he would have to pass sentence on his son just as he would on anyone else.

God is more just than any man is just. He is more righteous and more holy. Hence, when the law is violated, He has to pass sentence, no matter who the violator is. God loves men; nevertheless, He cannot overlook sin because of that love. Yet in His love He found a way to take care of the penalty: He, in the Person of His own blessed Son, took upon Himself man's sin and was paid the wages thereof; for "the wages of sin is death" (Romans 6:23). Thus, the law is fulfilled, the penalty paid, and "being now justified by his blood, we shall be saved from wrath through him" (Romans 5:9). "God commendeth his love toward us, in that, while we were yet sinners, Christ died for us" (Romans 5:8).

A personal worker asked a man, "Have you made peace with God?

"I never realized there was any war between us," he retorted.

The reason he did not realize there was war between him and God was that he did not recognize what sin is.

Sometimes a happy marriage relationship is broken

because of a serious difference between husband and wife. The offender goes to the other, confesses the wrong, tries to atone and to make peace; and the two become reconciled. But Jesus Christ, the innocent party, became sin and bore our penalty in order to reconcile us to God. Now we are at one with God; there is no difference standing between us—no division, no enmity. Concord is established, and we are united with Him in fellowship. The relationship is perfect because the act of atonement propitiated God's wrath.

Some people argue, "You must not speak about the wrath of God." They err. We should warn men about the wrath of God that abides on all who believe not the Son, and then point them to the love of God which spared not His own Son but gave Him a willing sacrifice for our salvation. God's Word declares, "He that believeth on the Son hath everlasting life: and he that believeth not the Son shall not see life; but the wrath of God abideth on him" (John 3:36).

When we erected the buildings on our present campus, we selected certain words to be carved over various buildings. On the library we put "The fear of the Lord is the beginning of wisdom" (Psalm 111:10).

The architect said, "I do not think you should talk about the fear of God. We need to talk about the love of God."

What does God's Word say? "The fear of the Lord tendeth to life: and he that hath it shall abide satisfied" (Proverbs 19:23). I, too, think we should speak of God's love. I would rather preach about the love of Christ than about any subject in the world. It is easy to understand how Mr. Moody preached a different sermon every night for six weeks on the text, "For God so loved the world, that he gave his only begotten Son, that whosoever believeth in him should not perish, but have everlasting life" (John 3:16). The love of God is inexhaustible and wonderful beyond comparison! Notwithstanding, there is a righteous fear that accompanies the right kind of love. A child ought to love his parents; but he does not properly love a parent whom he does not fear. This does not mean a cringing fear, but the kind of fear that draws back from hurting, injuring, or offending the parent. The same is true of husband and wife: each will be careful not to deliberately offend the other.

"He is a God-fearing man" is a term we rarely hear in our

day. A man ought to fear God—fear not only His judgment and hell, but also His anger against sin in the life of the Christian. "Whom the Lord loveth, He chasteneth" (Hebrews 12:6). If we love God, we will fear His chastening and will be careful to please Him. This is what we call "godly fear." If it is lacking in your life, there is something wrong in your relationship with your Saviour. Godly fear is begotten of respect. There is quite a difference between that kind of fear and the cringing fear that would make God a tyrant and His acts irrational.

A child might fear a drunken father; but that is not the kind of fear a child should feel for his parent. That fear comes because the parent is not rational and cannot be expected to act according to principle—how he acts depends on his state: if he is sober, he may be nice, whereas if he is drunk, he may abuse those around him. The kind of fear a child should have for his parent is the fear of causing undue concern and being a burden—the fear that motivates him to make a good record at school so that the money which has been invested in his education will not be wasted. This is an illustration on a small scale of the wholesome fear we are to manifest toward God.

The Bible warns us to "flee the wrath of God." It says that "it is a fearful thing to fall into the hands of the living God" (Hebrews 10:31). A sinner, guilty before God, should quake in his boots. America needs some strong preaching on hell such as that of Jonathan Edwards, who is said to have preached on hell with such force that people held onto the pews, for they could feel themselves falling into hell. Great revivals occurred under that type of preaching. Today, however, the trend is toward a sentimental, superficial emphasis upon love. There is a dearth of good, sensible, hard-hitting biblical sermons on hell and the wrath and judgment of God.

God is holy. He cannot tolerate sin. As sinners we could not come into His Presence. Our sins were a wall that had separated between us and God. But when Jesus Christ paid the price of sin, our sins were put away; and by faith in Him we became sinless in God's sight. He "redeemed us from the curse of the law, being made a curse for us" (Galatians 3:13); and He is "made unto us wisdom, and righteousness, and sanctification, and redemption" (I Corinthians 1:30). He vicariously took our place on a cross and died for us in fulfillment of the law's decree, "the soul that sinneth, it shall die" (Ezekiel 18:4, 20).

As God, Jesus Christ could not die. He had to take upon Himself the form of flesh in order to die for man. Having no sin of His own, Jesus Christ could take our sins; and in this sacrifice of Christ on the Cross, God's justice was fulfilled, the demand of the law was met, and God was able to be just and at the same time justify sinful man.

To *justify* means to declare a man under the law guiltless. When someone is tried and declared innocent in civil court, the case is dismissed and the person is justified; that is, justice has been met, and there is no longer a penalty over the accused. The Lord Jesus Christ, by dying on the Cross, satisfied God's justice and left us blameless before the law. All man has to do is accept what Christ has done—by faith believe it—and he becomes God's child. His sin is under the precious Blood of Jesus Christ, Who poured it out in payment for man's sin.

"Without shedding of blood is no remission" (Hebrews 9:22), says the Scripture. This principle is emphasized all the way through the Word of God. When Adam and Eve sinned in the garden, their efforts to cover themselves with aprons of fig leaves would not avail. God Himself had to kill beasts in order to get skins to cover their nakedness—the badge of their shame (Genesis 3:21). By this act God, in effect, was saying, "This is symbolic. The only hope for the covering of sinful man is by the shedding of blood. An innocent lamb—without spot and without blemish—has to die in order for you to be covered."

Wool can be provided for clothing without the death of the sheep. Wool is the hair of the animal, and it will grow back. But when you receive a diploma at graduation, a sheep had to die to provide that sheepskin parchment. The Lord covered Adam and Eve with hide, not hair. No doubt the hair was left on the hide, but the skin was the covering. It is significant that when John the Baptist preached in the wilderness he wore "raiment of camel's hair, and a leathern girdle about his loins" (Matthew 3:4). It was the hide that covered and that necessitated the death of the animal. John the Baptist was the prophet of judgment, and God's judgment demands shedding of the blood.

The Bible says, "For the life of the flesh is in the blood" (Leviticus 17:11). Man did not know that until a few years ago—relatively speaking. The ancients did not understand the circulation of the blood; they imagined that the blood was in some kind of cavity in the body. But the Bible explains it, because He Who planned the circulation of the blood also wrote the Word. Up until fairly modern times, doctors treated sickness by "letting" the blood. Today by transfusion blood is put into the veins. Too great a loss of blood can cause death. Blood is the essential life factor. As the heart beats, the blood courses through the veins and takes away the poisons; at the same time it carries nourishment to all the tissues and cells of the body.

Because the blood is the life element, Jesus Christ had to shed His blood just as those beasts at the edge of Eden had to give their lives for Adam and Eve. Before the fall, the pair had been robed with eternal light; the light of God was on them because God had made them in His own image. But when they sinned, the light went out; the glory left them, and they knew they were naked and had need of a covering. As Adam and Eve tried to make their own covering, so ever since man has been making the same attempt. By means of good works, church membership, charities, or something else, he seeks to satisfy God; but God labels all of man's righteousnesses "filthy rags" (Isaiah 64:6).

When God slew the animal and covered man, He symbolically pointed to Calvary where His Son—the Lamb slain from the foundation of the world (Revelation 13:8)—would lay down His life to save us from the penalty of sin. Every beast offered as a sacrifice in Old Testament times spoke of the perfect sacrifice of Christ on Calvary. And there were millions of them slain. From sunrise to sunset priests climbed to the top of the 40-foot-square altar at the Temple in Jerusalem and slew and burned the bodies of the animals!

The Bible says that it was not possible "that the blood of bulls and of goats should take away sins" (Hebrews 10:4)—that they could "never with those sacrifices which they offered year by year continually make the comers thereunto perfect" (v. 1). Why, then, did the Jews offer the sacrifices? They were a symbol of their faith that God would provide the sacrifice. God commanded it; and they obeyed. God is reasonable. He never asks us to do something we cannot do. If a Jew could afford a bullock, he brought one; but if he could not afford one, he brought a dove. In every case, the man who brought the sacrifice said by the act, "I recognize the principle that atonement is by blood"; and God counted it unto him for righteousness. It was a token of his faith in God's promise to provide a better sacrifice. On the Cross Jesus Christ "offered one sacrifice for sins for ever. . . . By one offering he hath perfected for ever them that are sanctified" (Hebrews 10:12, 14).

Mary Baker Eddy, the founder of Christian Science, in her book, *Science and Health, the Key to the Scriptures*, said that the blood of Jesus Christ was just as effective when it flowed in His veins as when it was shed on Calvary. There never was a worse lie than that. To know whether or not Mary Baker Eddy's work is sound, all one needs to do is read that one sentence in the light of God's statement "Without the shedding of blood is no remission." Any religion can be checked by its teaching with regard to Jesus Christ and His blood. If it does not give the proper place to God's Son and the proper emphasis to His shed blood, *it is a false religion*. The blood had to be shed, because "the life of the flesh is in the blood." His blood is the stream which flows from Calvary to wash away our sins and cover our guilt.

The purpose of His coming to earth was that He might "give his life a ransom for many" (Matthew 20:28). Other men are born to live; Jesus Christ was born to die. Throughout His earthly ministry He repeated, "Mine hour is not yet come" (John 2:4; 7:30). But in the shadow of the Cross He said: "The hour is at hand" (Matthew 26:18, 45; John 12:23; 13:1; 17:1). Jesus Christ is the everlasting God (Isaiah 9:6). He lived before there was a world (Colossians 1:16). He will live forever—He is the same "yesterday, today, and for ever" (Hebrews 13:8). Yet He came to earth "to lay down his life for the sheep" (John 10:15), "to seek and to save that which was lost" (Luke 19:10; I Timothy 1:15), to call not "the righteous, but sinners to repentance" (Matthew 9:13).

Those who emphasize the life and teachings of Jesus and neglect the blood of Jesus Christ are lost. The only hope for a sinner is the fact that God loved him and gave His Son; that the Son laid down His life a ransom for many—that He paid sin's penalty by dying on the Cross to save man from sin; and that faith in Him brings life—eternal life. "The blood of Jesus Christ his Son cleanseth us from all sin" (I John 1:7). There is no other cleansing. If Jesus Christ had not died, there would be no hope for any sinner. Had He come merely to teach men and nothing else, we would have new condemnation heaped upon us, for nobody would be able to live up to His teachings. The law condemns us because we are unable to keep it. It is "our schoolmaster to bring us unto Christ, that we might be justified by faith" (Galatians 3:24).

"Thou shalt love the Lord thy God with all thy heart, and with all thy soul, and with all thy mind. This is the first and great commandment. And the second is like unto it, Thou shalt love thy neighbor as thyself. On these two commandments hang all the law and the prophets." That is the teaching of Jesus Christ. What is it? Simply a recapitulation of the ten commandments. All are condemned under the ten commandments; and all would be condemned under that, too, because not one has loved God with all his heart, all his soul, and all his mind. There is no one who is not guilty of loving himself more than he loves somebody else. God's demand of perfection, whether it comes through the law of Moses or from the lips of Jesus Christ, condemns man. But whereas the teachings of Christ condemn, the death of Christ redeems. The words of Christ "are spirit, and they are life" (John 6:63); but no man can attain unto that life because man, as a sinner, cannot come up to the words that bring life. Only the blood of Jesus Christ gives life. It alone cleanses from sin. Man, believing and trusting therein, passes from death unto life. "By him all that believe are justified from all things, from which ye could not be justified by the law of Moses" (Acts 13:39). We should daily thank the Lord Jesus Christ for shedding His precious blood for us. Grace and truth come by Jesus Christ, and the truth of God's love and the evidence of His grace are found at Calvary.

In the New Testament the Lord institutes what He calls "the New Covenant" of His blood, the "new testament"—that is, the "new testimony," the new covenant between God and man. In the Old Testament the slain lamb or beast bespoke God's covenant to provide a perfect sacrifice. Today in the church when we take the cup which symbolizes the blood of Christ, we remember His death until He comes (I Corinthians 11:25, 26). Whenever a sacrifice was made in Old Testament times, the Jew was looking forward to the Cross. Whenever a born-again Christian partakes of the Lord's Supper and takes the cup, he looks back toward the Cross. The difference is that the Jew looked forward to the coming of the Messiah Who would pay the price for his sin, whereas we, though we look back to the Messiah Who came, Who was rejected, and Who died, also look forward to the One Who will come again. The death and glory of the Lord Jesus are intertwined in the Word of God. "If so be that we suffer with Him, that we may be also glorified together with Him" (Romans 8:17).

"I believe in . . . His vicarious atonement for the sins of mankind by the shedding of His blood on the Cross." To us has been given the "ministry of reconciliation: To wit, that God was in Christ, reconciling the world unto himself, not imputing their trespasses unto them; and hath committed unto us the word of reconciliation" (II Corinthians 5:18, 19).

"We are ambassadors for Christ." Our message is God-given. In Christ's stead, we beseech others "be ye reconciled to God."

THE RESURRECTION OF HIS BODY FROM THE TOMB

The bodily resurrection of our Lord is an essential part of the gospel. Anyone who does not believe that the same body that was laid in the tomb came out of the tomb does not believe the gospel. This is the gospel: "Christ died for our sins according to the scriptures; and he was buried, and that he rose again the third day according to the scriptures" (I Corinthians 15:3, 4). The gospel is "good news"; and it would not be good news if Christ had not risen from the dead. Good news is that the God-Man Who took the place of sinners and died on the Cross for their sins came forth from the grave in proof of the fact that He had conquered death and that the penalty of sin had been satisfactorily paid. If Jesus Christ be not bodily risen from the grave, His death on the Cross is of no avail. We are justified by faith—faith not only in the death, but also in the resurrection, of the Lord Jesus Christ. "Without shedding of blood is no remission" (Hebrews 9:22), and without the resurrection is no justification; for "Jesus our Lord . . . was delivered for our offences, and was raised again for our justification" (Romans 4:24, 25).

It is possible to judge a man's theology by the language he uses when speaking of sacred things. In these days we deal with people who neither say what they mean nor mean what they say. To those who deny the authority of God's Word, to the ecumenically minded—Protestant or non-Protestant—language is a means of deceiving people. This is true in the realm of politics also. Men are past masters at using words but do not mean what their words imply.

It reminds me of an incident in *Alice in Wonderland.* Alice, rebuking one of the other characters for some remark he had made, said, "That word doesn't mean that."

But he argued, "It means just what I choose it to mean."

It is a case of who is the boss—the person or the word. It is wrong to use words to mean something that they do not actually mean.

When true Christians speak of the resurrection of our Lord, they mean that His body came forth from the grave. To them, if there is no bodily resurrection, there is no resurrection at all. Liberals, on the other hand, speak of the "resurrection of Jesus" and say that it is "the teachings of Jesus living on in the lives of His followers," or that "spiritually, He is alive." Of course His teaching lives on in the lives of believers; but that is not resurrection. Moreover, the spirit is immortal, and therefore cannot die. Only the body is mortal and able to be touched by death. Obviously, if there is a resurrection from the dead, it must be a physical, bodily resurrection. How illogical is the thought that the spirit, which never dies, could rise from the dead.

If the body of Jesus Christ did not come forth from the grave, there is no hope of resurrection for any of us. But He is risen, and is "become the firstfruits of them that slept" (I Corinthians 15:20). The seed is planted in the ground, it germinates, the plant springs from the ground. The seed of life that was buried has come up from the soil, and "as in Adam all die, even so in Christ shall all be made alive." Jesus Christ was buried, but "He rose again the third day according to the scriptures." He was crucified a propitiation for our sins; He rose again the third day for our justification. By His resurrection He proved that His sacrifice was acceptable to God and that He was indeed the promised One. His death without His resurrection is incomplete. He had power to lay down His life, and He had power to take it again (John 10:18). His power to save men from sin is proven by His resurrection. We are cleansed by the blood, but our eternal life is assured by the resurrection of His body from the tomb. It is because He lives, that we, too, shall live (John 14:19).

The resurrection of our Lord is prophesied in the Old Testament. The psalmist said, "Thou wilt not leave my soul in hell; neither wilt thou suffer thine Holy One to see corruption" (Psalm 16:10). At Pentecost, Peter declared, "He seeing this before spake of the resurrection of Christ, that his soul was not left in hell, neither his flesh did see corruption" (Acts 2:31). Jesus Himself prophesied His resurrection: "From that time forth began Jesus to show unto his disciples, how that he must go into Jerusalem, and suffer many things of the elders and chief priests and scribes, and be killed, and be raised again the third day" (Matthew 16:21).

The resurrection is a cardinal truth of our Christian faith. Paul said, "If Christ be not risen, then is our preaching vain, and your faith is also vain . . . ye are yet in your sins" (I Corinthians 15:14, 17). If Jesus Christ did not rise from the dead, He was not the sinless Son of God. If He became a prisoner of death and went back to dust as other men go back to dust, then He was nothing but a mere man; and I have no hope of resurrection by trusting Him. Man's body is formed of the dust of the earth, and it is the law of nature that when a man dies, his body returns to dust; for sin produces corruption. But the Lord Jesus Christ was sinless; in His nature was no seed of corruption; hence His body was preserved from any touch of corruption. He became obedient unto death; yet death had no dominion over Him. If His body returned to dust, either He was not the Holy One of God, or else God's Word is not true; for God's Word promised that His Holy One should not see corruption. God raised up Jesus Christ, "having loosed the pains of death: because it was not possible that he should be holden of it" (Acts 2:24); and the body that came forth on resurrection morning was as spotless from the corruption of the tomb as the body that was taken down from the Cross, bathed, anointed, and buried in the borrowed tomb.

The whole record of the life of our Lord's incarnation ties together. He took upon Him the form of man; He suffered as a man; He rose again from the grave the firstfruits of them that sleep; He ascended on high; He will come back again; and throughout eternity He will wear the same body that took form in the womb of a virgin. The fact that He is seated with the Majesty on high in that same body and will keep it forever in heaven, is the proof of resurrection for ourselves. "If in this life only we have hope in Christ, we are of all men most miserable" (I Corinthians 15:19). I am glad the apostle did not stop there but continued with the definite affirmation. "But now is Christ risen from the dead."

Someone has said that the best attested fact of history is the bodily resurrection of the Lord Jesus Christ. He was seen alive of many witnesses. "He shewed himself alive after his passion by many infallible proofs, being seen . . . forty days" (Acts 1:3). Men touched Him; they felt the nail prints and put their hands in His side (John 20:27). They saw Him prepare and eat food (John 21:9-12). To the church at Corinth, Paul wrote of varied eye-witnesses to this great event: "He was seen of Cephas, then of the twelve: After that, he was seen of above five hundred brethren at once. . . . After that, he was seen of James; then of all the apostles. And last of all he was seen of me also, as of one born out of due time" (I Corinthians 15:5-8). In the presence of King Agrippa, Paul testified of the resurrection: "Having therefore obtained help of God, I continue unto this day, witnessing both to small and great, saying none other things than those which the prophets and Moses did say should come: That Christ should suffer, and that he should be the first that should rise from the dead" (Acts 26:22, 23). Stephen, when he was stoned to death, saw the heavens open and "the Son of man standing on the right hand of God" (Acts 7:56).

The risen body of our Lord was a glorified body, and in our resurrected bodies "We shall be like him" (I John 3:2). Our bodies will be different from the ones we have now; nevertheless, they will be the same bodies. The Word of God makes it very clear that in the resurrection of the dead, that which is sown in corruption shall come forth in incorruption; that which is sown in dishonor shall be raised in glory; that sown in weakness shall be raised in power; that which is sown a natural body shall be raised a spiritual body. "This corruptible must put on incorruption, and this mortal must put on immortality" (I Corinthians 15:53).

"We shall not all sleep, but we shall all be changed." By that is meant that not all men will have to experience death and resurrection to receive a glorified body. If we are alive when the Lord returns (and I believe some of us will be; I am not fixing dates and seasons, but I do not see how the world as it is in the hands of the men who rule it today can hold together much longer), we shall be translated. *Translate* is an interesting word to use in this connection. When something is changed from one language to another, it becomes subject to different rules of grammar. Suppose I translate something from English into Spanish. Spanish idiom is different from English idiom. For instance, in English we say, "My feet are cold." Translated into Spanish the same statement would be, "Tengo los pies frios," (I have the feet cold). Though the same truth is in both, it is in a different form. When we speak of the translation of the living saints at the coming of Christ, we mean that these mortal bodies—flesh, blood, and bone—will be translated into the likeness of His resurrection. The form may be somewhat different—not physically different, but different in the sense that the body now subject to the laws of earth will become a heavenly body and be subject to the laws of heaven.

On the day that our Lord arose, the disciples, fearing the Jews, were assembled in an upper room behind closed doors. Suddenly the Lord appeared in their midst. The first glimpse of Him terrified the disciples; they thought they were seeing a spirit. But our Lord said, "Why are ye troubled? and why do thoughts arise in your hearts? Behold my hands and my feet, that it is I myself: handle me, and see; for a spirit hath not flesh and bones, as ye see me have" (Luke 24:38, 39). It is strange how men will take refuge from the supernatural in the superstitious. What could be more natural than that the God Who is the giver of life, the Lord of life, the Eternal One, the Everlasting God, should come forth from a grave? The miracle is not that He should rise again, but that He was willing to be obedient unto death for our sins. To those to whom He is only a spirit there is no reality of experience, no divine purpose and anointing in life. Christianity is centered in a living, divine Person Whose resurrected body could be touched, handled, and seen; and this is one of the great differences between the religion of Jesus Christ and all other religions.

The resurrection of the Lord is an infinitely important truth. It matters whether or not we believe it. It matters whether or not it is true. Unless He rose again the third day according to the Scripture, He is not able to save men; for He Himself is bound by death and subject to death. Only the Lord of life can give life. The risen Lord is the power and victory of the church and the answer to a sinner's need. Men can only know the resurrection power of Jesus Christ as they see it revealed in the life of a transformed child of God. Until the Lord returns, it is our obligation as Christians to manifest in our lives the witness that He is risen from the dead.

"They which live should not henceforth live unto themselves, but unto him which died for them, and rose again" (II Corinthians 5:15).

HIS POWER TO SAVE MEN FROM SIN

H*is power to save men from sin* has been proven in the lives of all who have trusted Him. When Jesus Christ died on the Cross, it was for a definite purpose: to pay the price of sin. Man had sinned and had sold himself a slave to the devil. But God's own Son, in the likeness of sinful flesh, shed His precious blood to pay the price of the sin and to redeem the slave. That the price was acceptable unto God was proven by "the resurrection of His body from the tomb." "For if, when we were enemies, we were reconciled to God by the death of his Son, much more, being reconciled, we shall be saved by his life" (Romans 5:10). "Wherefore he is able also to save them to the uttermost that come unto God by him, seeing he ever liveth to make intercession for them" (Hebrews 7:25).

Being saved from sin does not mean simply that the past is blotted out by the Blood. That is only part of it. Salvation includes being saved from the power of sin now, and eventually from the very presence of sin. We might say that there are three aspects of salvation.

The first great aspect is that He saves us from the *guilt* of sin. That takes care of the past. The Blood of Christ applied to a man's heart cleanses that heart from all sin and makes it as white in God's sight as if there never had been any sin. "Come now, and let us reason together, saith the Lord: though your sins be as scarlet, they shall be as white as snow; though they be red like crimson, they shall be as wool" (Isaiah 1:18). The effect of past sin may continue, however; for a sinful act, once committed, cannot be called back. One of the characteristics of sin is that its results live on. Suppose, for example, that while yet in your sins you had killed a man. Upon your acceptance of His Son as your Saviour, God would forgive the sin; but He would not restore life to the man you murdered. Again, suppose that through sinful living you sustained a crippling injury. God would forgive the sin that caused it; nevertheless, the effect of the sin upon your body—the blind eye, the maimed leg, or the wrecked physique—would remain. But whereas the effects of sin upon ourselves and upon others live on, the sin itself, as far as any guilt before God is concerned, is as though it had never been. This assurance we have from God's Word: "I have blotted out, as a thick cloud, thy transgressions, and, as a cloud, thy sins" (Isaiah 44:22; Colossians 2:13, 14). Your "sins and iniquities will I remember no more" (Hebrews 10:17). "As far as the east is from the west, so far hath he removed our transgressions from us" (Psalm 103:12).

It is said that we live in an expanding universe—that the east and west are constantly moving farther away from each other. I hope that is true, for it means that by the grace of God my sins are farther away from me today than they were yesterday and that they will continue to be put farther and farther behind me. How wonderful that God, when He forgives sin, forgets sin; that when we put our trust in His only begotten Son, Whom He sent to atone for our sins, the record becomes absolutely spotless and the page clean; and that at the judgment, believers will not have to answer for the guilt of sin. There will be judgment for reward, of course, at which time our works will be judged (Romans 14:10; I Corinthians 3:11-15; I Corinthians 4:5; Colossians 3:24, 25; II Timothy 4:8; Revelation 22:12). "Every man's work shall be made manifest ... and the fire shall try ... of what sort it is. If any man's work abide ... he shall receive a reward" (I Corinthians 3:13, 14). But that is an altogether different matter. Our sins have been judged at Calvary; our past is blotted out. "Being now justified ["just-as-if-I'd never sinned," someone has aptly defined it] by his blood, we shall be saved from wrath through him" (Romans 5:9); for "there is therefore now no condemnation to them which are in Christ Jesus, who walk not after the flesh, but after the Spirit" (Romans 8:1).

The second aspect of His saving us from sin has to do with the present: He saves us from the *power* of sin in this present world. God's will is that Christians seek to be perfect, even as the Father in Heaven is perfect (Matthew 5:48); and He can release us from the power of sin in our lives. He gives us the definite promise that sin shall not have dominion over us (Romans 6:14). A drunkard, by simple faith in the Lord Jesus Christ, can be forgiven of his sins and have his past blotted out. Moreover, if he trusts God for it, he can have victory over the "thirst for drink" so that he no longer is bound by its power. So also with the man who was unclean: he can be made clean and given the victory over his sinful appetite through the days that follow. Having been crucified with Christ, the life now lived in the flesh is lived by the faith of the Son of God, who loved us, and gave Himself for us (Galatians 2:20), whose blood cleanseth us from all unrighteousness (I John 1:9), and whose Word abiding in us makes us strong to overcome the wicked one (I John 2:14).

THE NEW BIRTH THROUGH THE REGENERATION BY THE HOLY SPIRIT

"Except a man be born again, he cannot see the kingdom of God" (John 3:3). These words of Jesus are clear and emphatic. Taken in context, they state a fact that is stressed throughout the Word of God—that is, that man is born in sin (Psalm 51:5) and in his natural state cannot please God (Romans 8) nor understand the things of God (I Corinthians 2:14). Nicodemus, to whom these words were spoken, was a "ruler of the Jews," a "master in Israel." He addressed Jesus as "Good Master," and acknowledged Him "a teacher come from God." But that was not enough: he needed to be "born again." Jesus said to him, "Except a man be born of water and of the Spirit, he cannot enter into the kingdom of God."

Some men interpret this passage to mean that baptism is essential to salvation. That is not what our Lord meant. He was speaking of two births—the physical birth by which we come into the world, and the spiritual birth by which we come into the family of God and become joint-heirs with His Son, Jesus Christ. As with the physical birth, so with the spiritual birth; there is some mystery surrounding it. Jesus explained it, "The wind bloweth where it listeth, and thou hearest the sound thereof, but canst not tell whence it cometh, and whither it goeth: so is every one that is born of the Spirit." Paul said, "The things of God knoweth no man, but the Spirit of God. Now we have received ... the spirit which is of God; that we might know the things that are freely given us of God" (I Corinthians 2:11, 12). Because we have received Jesus Christ, have believed on His Name, power has been given us to become the sons of God. In other words, we have experienced the second birth, which is "not of blood, nor of the will of the flesh, nor of the will of man, but of God" (John 1:12, 13).

Having been born of God, we are children of God. In our hearts is the Spirit of His Son "crying, Abba, Father" (Galatians 4:6). A child has certain characteristics common to the family into which he is born. He has some of the appetites of his parents. New England families are supposed to like clam chowder and Boston baked beans. Southerners eat turnip greens, grits, and fried chicken. In China rice is a staple diet. Similarly, a man who is born of God will manifest characteristics of his Father. He will love the things that God loves and will hate the things that God hates. "In this the children of God are manifest, and the children of the devil: Whosoever doeth not righteousness is not of God, neither he that loveth not his brother" (I John 3:10).

The man who has not experienced the new birth is on his way to hell; for no man can see God unless he is born of the Spirit of God. Some people mistake reformation for regeneration. These are not at all the same. Reformation says to a man, "You can conquer and rise above what you have been in the past. Whereas you have been a thief, you can reform and become an honest man." It is possible for a man with a strong will—especially if he has the proper help from outside sources—to reform. Notwithstanding, he still carries the guilt of his past. Reformation does not take care of the past; it merely helps a person do somewhat better in the future. But no man is saved by determining to do better—by simply changing his outlook; for basically no man's outlook ever changes save as does the man himself; and that change is brought about by regeneration.

Regeneration means a "renewing of life." It is a synonym for "a new life." By its miracle, a man once dead in trespasses and sin becomes "a new man in Christ Jesus." A new heart replaces the old stony heart, and a new spirit is put within (Ezekiel 11:19, 20).

Sometimes when we ask a person to accept Christ, we say to him, "Will you give your heart to the Lord?" The expression is all right, but actually God does not want the old heart; for it is sinful and black—"the fountainhead of all evil" (Mark 7:21). What God wants to do is take away the old heart and put in its place an honest and good heart (Luke 8:15) of right principles which will bear the fruit of right actions to the glory of God.

When a man is born again, the grace of God imparts to him a new nature. God's Word describes it, "If any man be in Christ, he is a new creature: old things are passed away; behold, all things are become new" (II Corinthians 5:17). A better translation could be, "If any man be in Christ, he is a new *creation.*" Paul wrote to the Ephesians, "We are his workmanship, created in Christ Jesus unto good works" (2:10). The meaning of the original, I am told, is that we are His creation in the sense that we are like a poem created by a poet. When by His grace we experience the new birth, we are God's workmanship not only in the sense that we are made by Him into a new creature, but also in the sense that we are His expression of His own deep emotions of love as a poem is the expression of the heart of the poet. That is a wonderful thought!

Until a man is born again, he is dead unto God (Ephesians 2); and being dead, he cannot please God. As far as spiritual things are concerned, an unregenerated man cannot comprehend spiritual truths. Indeed, they are foolishness to him (I Corinthians 2:14). No wonder John said, "He that knoweth God heareth us" (I John 4:6). Those who knew God heard the apostle because he was dealing with the eternal things of God. The heart of any born-again person naturally responds to whatever is of God, for he has God's nature imparted to him by the miracle of regeneration. If you do not delight in the Word of God, if it does not say much to you as you meditate therein, if your heart does not respond to the spiritual and is not thrilled when people exalt the Lord Jesus Christ, if the discussion of spiritual truths bores you, you had better be concerned as to whether or not you have spiritual life.

You may not know the time or the place of your second birth, but you should be sure that there has been a time and a place. I once knew a man who had been left on the doorstep of a family when he was only two months old. He did not know when nor where nor to whom he had been born. But he was aware of physical existence and had contact with the world about him. Your new birth could have occurred when you were quite young. Nevertheless, if you have eternal life, there will be certain evidences that you have been born again. First of all, the Spirit bears witness with your spirit that you are a child of God (Romans 8:16). Then, you may know that you have passed from death unto life because you "love the brethren" (I John 3:14). If you prefer the company of sinners to fellowship with Christians, you have not been born again. However, you can be born again right now. The Lord has promised, "Him that cometh to me I will in no wise cast out" (John 6:37). He is the way, the truth, and the life: no man comes to the Father but by Him (John 14:6).

Though we are new creatures in Christ, we are still in the flesh and must fight against the temptations of that flesh. Paul realized the presence of the old nature, for he said, "When I would do good, evil is present with me" (Romans 7:21). Then he cried, "Who can deliver me from the body of this death?" For people who considered themselves civilized, the Romans had a very cruel and wicked custom. When two men were taken in the same crime, one was executed and the other one left alive. The body of the dead man was tightly bound to the body of the live criminal—cheek to cheek, arm to arm, chest to chest—until the corruption of the dead body caused the death of the other criminal. No more horrible form of torment could ever be imagined! That is exactly what Paul had in mind when he cried, "Who shall deliver me from the body of this death?" Our new nature is bound in the old, corrupt body. We are two creatures—the new man, and the old man. The new is in the old, and there is constant warfare between the two. But "we have this treasure in earthen vessels, that the excellency of the power may be of God, and not of us." He gives grace, and He also gives strength. We could never make it alone.

THE GIFT OF ETERNAL LIFE BY THE GRACE OF GOD

The gift of eternal life by the grace of God is included for this reason: Some people teach that a man can become an heir of eternal life through some effort of his own. That is false doctrine. The Word of God makes it plain that eternal life is a free gift of God—that it is "by grace . . . through faith . . . not of works, lest any man should boast" (Ephesians 2:8, 9).

By the *grace* of God is meant "unmerited favor." Grace and mercy are not the same. God is a God of mercy, but He is also a God of grace. If we earn something and receive it, it is not of grace. The man who works and is paid a salary for the work does not receive the money by grace: it is remuneration for service rendered. The man earned it; hence he is entitled to it. Grace, however, is that which is extended to one who is wholly undeserving of it. It is God's favor, God's forgiveness, extended to those who have no claim on God's mercy. It is that to which we are in no wise entitled, but which is given as an act of special favor. If we received our just dues, we would receive judgment and hell and would forever abide under the wrath of God; for sin deserves those things. "The wages of sin is death" (Romans 6:23).

A man's attitude toward sin depends upon what he is. For example, one who has lived a wicked life would not consider it much of a sin to read some modern novel that is vulgar and degrading. He is a hardened sinner who is accustomed to doing all the evil things mentioned in the book; therefore his conscience would not be troubled by reading it. But to a young and innocent person who has been reared in the Christian home and protected from the evils described therein, the novel would be terrible, because his own heart is pure. God is infinitely holy, absolutely pure, and wholly righteous. To Him sin is sin; and it is terrible, no matter how small it may seem in the eyes of man. "All our righteousnesses are as filthy rags" in His sight (Isaiah 64:6); and if He gave us what we deserved, we would receive His wrath, His judgment, and His punishment. But because He is a God of love and grace, He gives to us the gift of eternal life through Jesus Christ our Lord (Romans 6:23). We are saved because Christ died for our sins, God offered us a pardon, and we as poor miserable sinners accepted it by faith.

"This is eternal life," says our Lord: "that they might know thee the only true God, and Jesus Christ, whom thou hast sent" (John 17:3). "He that believeth on the Son hath everlasting life: and he that believeth not the Son shall not see life; but the wrath of God abideth on him" (John 3:36; John 4:14). We are not saved by believing Christ *and* going to confession; by believing Christ *and* going to church; by believing Christ *and* praying to the Virgin Mary and the saints. We are saved because we have believed in Christ. We have reached out a hand of faith and accepted God's free gift.

Suppose a man is given a ticket for a Caribbean cruise. What would you think of him, if having a ticket that entitles him to all the luxuries of the liner, he boards the ship, reports to the captain, and asks, "Which deck do I scrub first? I have to work my passage." God's free gift entitles us to everything that God has for His children; and we do not have to scrub one deck to get it. Of course, in appreciation for the gift, and because we cannot help ourselves, we will try to bring others to receive the gift also. We will want to be a good witness for God and do those things which please Him. We will not want to do anything that will grieve or hurt the One Who made it possible for us to enjoy all the riches of salvation. But the gift itself is free. All is of God.

If we did any work for salvation, it would be of work and not of grace; if we paid for salvation, it would be of purchase and not of grace. But the *gift* of eternal life is by the *grace* of God. We did not deserve it, and God did not give it to us because He felt that we were in the least degree entitled to it. Rather, He loved us so much that He gave it to us in spite of the fact that we did not deserve it.

CONCLUSION

In closing these messages, perhaps it would be wise to explain the answer to a question we are often asked: "Why do you not include a statement with regard to the Second Coming of our Lord?"

The Bob Jones University Creed was written by a very godly man who was both a journalist and a preacher. He wrote it on the back of an envelope years ago when my father was first planning to found a school that would honor God's Son and God's Word and train young people to go out in complete dedication to His service and will. Many people had been asked to write the Creed; but Sam Small was the first to submit one that was brief, clear, and to the point in combining the fundamentals of the Christian faith to which all Bible-believing Christians subscribe.

Not all people who believe the Book and want to honor it agree on the interpretation of all that is contained therein. For instance, all people do not agree as to method of baptism. Some of us believe that scriptural baptism is by immersion only. Others—equally sincere and equally devoted to the Book—believe that the Bible is not clear as to what the mode of baptism really is. Still others go so far as to say they do not believe that the Bible teaches any form of baptism for this dispensation, since the time of the apostles. Therefore, in our Creed we cover only those fundamentals which are so clear in the Word of God as to admit to no differences of interpretation.

With regard to the Lord's return, the position of the Administration and Bible faculty of the University is as follows: We believe that God's Word clearly teaches that Jesus Christ will come for His Bride *before* the Tribulation—that the church will not go through that terrible time. We believe that the Bible teaches that the Lord will return *before* the Millennium—that He will establish His kingdom on the earth and will bring about the thousand years of peace. I, personally, do not see how anyone can read the Bible and hold any other interpretation of this blessed event. However, it is always difficult for one of strong convictions to recognize the fact that others may reasonably differ with him.

The Word of God is clear on the matter of separation from infidelity. So also with believers' obedience to the will and Word of God. But there are other points which good men can interpret differently; and the Second Coming is one of these points.

As far as the testimony of Bob Jones University is concerned, we do not go beyond this Creed. We agree that "whatever the Bible says is so"; but beyond that point we will not argue. Some people believe that it is possible to lose their salvation; others believe that "once saved, they are always saved." Our institution does not argue these points. Our position is that the important thing is to *have* salvation. Therefore, we seek to point men to Him Who is the way to eternal life. To those who love to argue for their interpretation of God's Word on this point, we say that if it is possible to lose salvation, a Christian should stay close to the Lord so that he will not lose it; and that if he cannot lose salvation, he needs to be busy winning souls so that others can enjoy his security with him.